Yates, Janelle.

Zora Neale Hurston.

DATE			
FEB 02			

UNSUNG AMERICANS

ZORA NEALE HURSTON

A Storyteller's Life

by Janelle Yates

With Illustrations by David Adams

WARD HILL PRESS

Published by
Ward Hill Press
PO Box 04-0424
Staten Island, NY 10304
(718) 816-9449

Cover design by Jim O'Grady and Diana Yates

LIBRARY OF CONGRESS CATALOG CARD NUMBER 91-65559

ISBN 0-9623380-1-X Paper
ISBN 0-9623380-3-6 Library edition

Contents

UNSUNG AMERICANS

Other books in this series include:

Chief Joseph: Thunder Rolling Down From the Mountains

Dorothy Day: With Love for the Poor

For Alex and Adrienne

1

Traveling

When Zora Neale Hurston took her first trip out of Eatonville, Florida, she was still a small child. Her father had to travel to Sanford for the day, and Sanford was just far enough away to require a train to get there. He was taking Zora's older brother Bob because he needed some extra help. He was taking Zora because her Mama told him to, even though Zora seemed to get on his nerves most of the time. But she was excited. She had never seen a train before.

Years later Zora Hurston would travel widely across the United States and West Indies and make her home in many different places. But on the day of her first real journey, she and her brother and father walked the mile or so to the rail station in Maitland and stood together on the platform. As they waited, Papa talked with a friend while Bob listened and Zora stared up the track. After a while, a small shadow appeared in the distance and started moving toward them, getting bigger as it approached and making a strange noise. To Zora, the rhythmic churning of the train's engine sounded harsh and foreign. It seemed to be chanting the same phrase over and over, shooting steam out of its head as it moved, but she couldn't understand a word. And the closer the train got, the more it sounded like roaring wind with words in the background. It was certainly not what she had expected. It was a huge, one-eyed monster hurtling down the track! And when it finally stopped and stood panting horribly in the station, Zora turned and ran for home.

Then everybody started yelling.

"Stop her! Catch her!"

That just made her run all the harder.

Zora Hurston was never a coward, even as a child. In fact, among her family and friends, she was known for her bravery. She was the only girl in Eatonville who could take a beating from the boys without shedding a tear, and she was always sitting up on the gate-post in front of her house shouting hellos to friends and strangers alike. She disappeared into the woods alone often enough that her mother thought someone had cast a spell on her. Zora was spirited, restless and curious — but certainly no coward! So it was quite an occurrence when she bolted and ran from the train.

Having longer legs than Zora, Bob soon headed her off, cornered her in a local store and dragged her back to the platform. Then he and Papa hoisted her onto the train, laughing as hard as they could considering all the running they'd done. In fact, Zora noticed, everyone on the train was laughing. Embarrassed, she slumped down in one of the seats by the window and tried to pretend they were laughing at someone else. But then the porter brought her some candy and said she had hurt the train's feelings, so she began to relax and look around.

On the inside, the train was lovely! The seat cushions were covered in soft red fabric and the metal around the windows gleamed as though it had just been polished. The car was clean and comfortable, with a row of windows down each side that flooded the interior with light.

In a few minutes, the train began to move again, in a slow, hesitant whisper at first but then faster and with a stronger voice. Zora stared out the window and watched trees and ponds slide past. She wondered how far the train would go if she stayed on it forever. Maybe to the edge of the world, where the land and the sky joined together. Maybe that's what it was chanting — its destination! Zora leaned back and closed her eyes and listened.

2

Eatonville

When Zora was born in 1891, Eatonville was only five years old. It was founded by a man named Joe Clarke, one of the first people in south central Florida to believe that black folks could govern themselves without any help from white men.

But it took the assistance of Captain Eaton, a white man from Maitland, to buy land a mile or so down the road and build a meeting hall. When the town got started, the people named it after Captain Eaton — for all his help — but they elected Joe Clarke mayor. And when the state of Florida granted it a charter in 1886, Eatonville became the first all-black township incorporated in North America.

The Hurston family lived in a large, eight-room house surrounded by flowers and fruit trees. Behind their house was a big vegetable garden, and a little beyond it the chicken coops. In front gardenia bushes framed the path to the gate, and a wood fence divided the yard from the dirt road that ran through town. A long, partially covered porch spanned the width of the house. Some evenings Lucy Hurston sat outside in her rocker and sewed while her children tumbled and wrestled in the grass. She had eight: six boys and two girls. Zora was the fifth oldest but the youngest daughter.

Zora's parents were about as different from one another as they could get. John Hurston was tall and muscular —

one of the handsomest men in town, everybody said. He was also a Baptist preacher, and a good one, too. When he stood in front of his church every week, looking out over crowded benches and expectant faces, his loud, melodic voice always moved at least a few people to tears. Although he had his share of enemies outside the church, inside he was its undisputed leader.

Lucy Potts Hurston, on the other hand, was tiny and delicate-looking. But what she lacked in size and strength, she made up for in spirit. Like her husband she was a natural leader, only she didn't waste time choosing words. At home she was the boss, and none of the children questioned her authority. Her husband lost his temper and threatened her at times, but he was secretly afraid of her. And since she was smarter than he was, he turned to her for advice whenever he had a serious problem to solve.

Like their parents, Zora and her older sister Sarah were opposites. From the moment she was born, Sarah was Papa's favorite child. He showered her with gifts and saw that she was prettily dressed in lace and ruffles. And he was always comparing her to Zora — who came up short time after time.

"Why you runnin' around like a wild goat?" he'd say. "Go wash up and behave yourself! Can't you act like your sister?"

Then Mama would jump in to defend her. "Leave her alone John Hurston! She's my child! And if I think she needs correcting I'll be the one to say so!"

Naturally this made the two sisters a little jealous of each other. But since it had always been that way, they didn't dwell too much on their differences. Besides, they had six brothers, and the older ones loved to torment them.

One of Zora's favorite pastimes was playing tag in the yard, even though her brothers always caught her. That was most of the fun, after all. She'd hide alongside the house and run out with a loud whoop whenever one of them came into view.

The Hurstons were not rich by any means. To make ends meet, Papa had to work at construction jobs during the week because preaching never paid enough. But the garden and fruit trees always yielded plenty to eat. When the family needed meat, Papa killed one of the chickens or caught a few fish in the lake. Every once in a while, when he had to travel to Orlando on business, he brought back a roast for supper, and that was a special occasion.

In Eatonville, Zora never thought of herself as a little black child. She was simply Zora, John and Lucy's daughter. If she had hopes and dreams about the future, so what? So did everyone else. She never learned, as many black children in the South had to, that only white children could expect rosy futures. In Eatonville, she felt happy and secure.

Of course there were regular arguments with Papa, who thought she was a little too bold. Since his mother had been a slave, John Hurston was always a little fearful of white folks, and not without good reason. He knew a lot of them couldn't stand the idea of treating blacks as equals, so whenever Zora told him any of her plans for the future, like the time she said she was going to buy a pony and ride it to the end of the world, he lost his temper.

"You know what's goin' to happen when white folks gets wind of your crazy ideas?" he'd say. "The world is goin' to hit you like a slap in the face! Don't you be goin' round tellin' people them fool stories!"

But Zora would just giggle. "Oh, Papa!" she'd say, shaking her head at his foolishness. "Nobody's goin' to bother me." Before she knew it Papa was yelling and pounding on things, and he kept it up until Mama came and told him to stop.

Mama was the anchor of Zora's world. She was always there to listen when Zora had a problem or a story to tell. And she was glad her children could grow up in Eatonville away from the watchful eyes of whites. She encouraged them all to "jump at de sun," to aim for what they wanted even if it seemed impossible. As Zora explained later, "we might not land on the sun, but at least we would get off the ground."

In Zora's day, south central Florida was still very wild. White men built themselves tall, fancy houses and rode around in well-kept carriages and dressed in fine clothes. But their towns were surrounded by thick, swamp-like forests. Inside some of these forests it was as black as midnight at noon. And alligators still bellowed from the shores of the lakes at night. In Maitland, if a person wanted to walk down the street after dark, it was necessary to carry a lantern to keep from tripping over an alligator or one of the bulky, rope-like snakes coiled on the ground. And the roads! They were just ruts worn in the dirt! When a tree got in the way, the ruts just zigzagged around it. Every once in a while someone might get fed up and chop a tree down, but then wagons just bounced over the stump, rattling their passengers' teeth like gourd drums.

In Eatonville, the centerpiece of the town was Mayor Joe Clarke's store porch. In the evenings, after working all

day, the men gathered there to swap stories and comment on their neighbors. Sometimes the women would stop and share the conversation. Talking was a familiar pastime all over the South before television arrived and began pulling people into their houses away from their neighbors. Common folk across the country gathered in the evenings to talk. In Eatonville, they did it at Joe Clarke's store while a group of children played nearby.

As a child, Zora gravitated toward the store like everyone else. The only problem was that she didn't have many occasions to go there. Mama liked her to stay close to home, even though she hardly ever did. But sometimes Mama sent her to buy something or mail a letter, and Zora would take a long time to do it so she could hear as much of the talking as possible. Once the men started telling stories, it got to be a kind of contest to see who was the best. Most of the stories they told were old ones about familiar characters: Br'er Rabbit, Sis Snail, the Squinch Owl and, of course, God and the Devil. But every time a store-porch talker told one of these tales, he'd change it a little — put his fingerprints on it, you might say. And when they discussed each other, the talkers made it a practice to exaggerate as much as possible. The bigger the exaggeration the better. Instead of just calling somebody "ugly," a talker would accuse him of being *"so ugly they had to spread a sheet over his head at night so sleep could slip up on him."* Then they'd all laugh and think up something else. Anything and anyone were fair game.

One man might say he'd seen a fierce wind on the East Coast. *"It blowed a crooked road straight and blowed a well up out de ground and blowed and blowed until it scattered de days of de week so bad till Sunday didn't come till late Tuesday evenin'."* Another would explain that *"when it lightnings, de angels is peepin' in de lookin' glass; when it thunders, they's rollin' out de rain-barrels; and when it rains, somebody done dropped a barrel or two and bust it."* That would get them warmed up for the longer pieces.

As an adult, Zora wrote, "Nothing that God ever made is the same thing to more than one person. That is natural. There is no single face in nature, because every eye that looks upon it sees it from its own angle." From an early age, Zora saw magic in the world around her. When she was small, she believed she was the moon's special friend, since it followed her whenever she ran down the road, and waited overhead when she climbed trees or sat on the gate-post. And when there was no magic to behold in the world, she invented her own. When she passed a man on the road with leathery dark fingers clenched like claws, she imagined he

was the secret king of the alligators down in the lake. At night, she believed, he became an alligator himself and slithered down the road to the water to issue commands. Every morning, just before dawn, he crawled home and became a man again. Anybody unlucky enough to cross his path at night would surely become his victim. When a local woman fell in the lake, Zora believed the alligator-man was responsible. He must have threatened to do much worse if she ever told anyone about him, because the woman claimed she had only tripped.

When Zora stared down the road in front of her house, she knew the world sprawled around her held boundless other mysteries. That world drew her like a magnet. Since Florida weathers are mild and summers make the houses hot, Zora stayed outdoors as much as possible. Rarely did she wear shoes. She liked the feel of the grass curled tenderly beneath her feet, and the soft, powdery surface of the road. She liked to run down it as fast as she could with her arms out, trying to fly. She liked to wander into the woods and sit, quietly watching the animals. After they got used to her presence, they would venture out of their hiding places. Once a small squirrel paused a few feet away and sniffed in Zora's direction, then stood trembling all over. In the shadows of the woods, its golden fur looked dark. Then, as quickly as it had come, the squirrel turned and fled, vanishing in a flash of greenery up the rough surface of a tree trunk.

Sometimes Zora would climb a tree to stare out at the horizon and wonder about it. She was curious to know how it looked up close. Was there a seam where the land and sky came together? Or a gap running along the rim of the world? She was determined to discover these things one day, the sooner the better.

On summer nights, when it was time to wash up and get in bed, Zora would sometimes discover a fine layer of dust coating her arms and legs and drizzled across the top of her hair. She never noticed it outdoors, only when she stood in front of the wash basin. It seemed mysteriously beautiful. Mama once said somebody had sprinkled travel dust on their doorstep the day Zora was born, and Zora knew it was true. It sought her out time after time, falling invisibly out of the sky and clinging gently but stubbornly to her smooth brown skin.

3

Color

During the Civil War, Abraham Lincoln declared the slaves in all the Southern states free. But even after the war ended, life for the freed slaves contained many of the same miseries it had always held. After any war, a lot of hatred remains between the winners and losers. And the Civil War left a lot of hatred in its wake, since it was fought between citizens of the same country.

Zora Hurston was born almost 30 years after the war ended. But because she was black, it affected her life in many ways. One year after the war, a group of Southern veterans formed an organization called the Ku Klux Klan. Although it started out as a social club, it quickly became a terrifying symbol of racial hatred. Its primary aim was to keep black men from voting. So its members, all white men, wore masks and white cardboard hats and covered their clothes and horses with white sheets to hide their identities. They rode through the night terrorizing black families, and murder was a common outcome. There were other violent mobs, too, besides the Ku Klux Klan; sometimes they dressed like members of the Klan to disguise themselves.

A few years later, Southern whites began passing laws called "black codes" forbidding blacks to own guns, serve on juries, or go to school with whites. When black men tried to vote, they were threatened with violence, given examinations called “literacy tests” that were impossible to pass, or asked to pay a “poll tax” they couldn’t afford. Although slavery had been abolished, Southern whites soon had complete control again. And they were full of hate from the war. Many of them directed this hate at the black men, women and children who lived around them.

Since slavery had been practiced in most parts of Florida, these problems sprang up throughout the state. But in south central Florida, where Zora grew up, the violence wasn’t as severe. That was because south central Florida was developed *after* the war, by white men from all over the world. These men treated their black neighbors a little better than Southern whites did. Nevertheless, hatred flourished.

One evening in Eatonville, a group of Papa’s friends came to the Hurston house looking for him. Zora listened to them talk among themselves on the porch, but she couldn’t understand what they were saying. She did notice that Mama was acting awful strange, standing in the doorway without talking, her fingers tightly gripping the door frame. After a few minutes, Papa came in, took his rifle, and headed out the door to join the men. He told Mama to take the children into her bedroom and stay there until he returned. Mama immediately extinguished all the lights and herded Zora and the others into her room, where they sat in darkness along the floor. Mama wouldn’t talk much except to say the men had gone to help a friend in trouble.

Later Zora learned what really happened. Some of the men had heard screams coming from the woods outside town. Since Jim Watson wasn’t home when they started checking houses, they assumed he was the one in trouble. In the South, it was not unusual for a white mob to grab a black man or boy off his path and beat him severely. Many times, after the beating, the victim was hung by the neck, even set on fire. This crime was called lynching, and it was widespread. Between 1889 and 1903, there were an average of two lynchings each week in the South. In most cases, the murderers were never punished. Around Eatonville, this crime was much less common, but it still occurred. So when they heard screams, the men went off to try and save Jim Watson.

As Zora and her brothers and sister crouched in the dark bedroom, the night seemed unusually still. Hardly a breeze shook the curtains. Even the insects seemed to have suspended their ceaseless calling. Zora strained as hard as she could to hear every sound. Mama was whispering hurried prayers in the corner. And Zora's brothers, who were always jabbing at each other trying to provoke a fight, sat still and silent. After what seemed like a year of nights, Zora heard a sound in the distance. Soon she could discern the tramp of feet down the road, and the voices of men. Then she heard her father's voice. He was laughing!

Mama jumped up and ran to the door to meet him. "John?" She seemed to want to say more, but got only the one word out. "John?"

"Hey, Lulu! It's alright, you can light the lanterns again!"

Mama went into the kitchen and struggled to make light. When she came out again, Zora saw that her arm was trembling. The lantern threw a wobbly pattern across the porch and illuminated the lower half of Papa's face.

"Ah, baby, it's alright," Papa said, taking the lantern from his wife. "It was just some white folks beating up on one of their own. Jim Watson is home safe. Ain't nothing else to worry about."

Some of the men, who had been standing at the bottom of the steps, departed for their own homes. But a few stayed and sat with Papa on the porch long past the time that Zora finally went to bed. As she drifted into sleep, she could still hear them laughing.

In Eatonville, where everyone was black, Zora never gave much thought to skin color. But as she grew older and ventured further into the world, she discovered that most people were very conscious of color. They had two basic beliefs about it: white was good; anything else was bad. If your skin was white, it meant you were destined to control the world. If it was black, it meant you had to follow orders.

In many places, these beliefs were so strong and ran so deep that even some black people adopted them. Zora thought this was crazy. In Eatonville, on Joe Clarke's store porch, she had heard the real truth about skin color. It went like this.

God did not make folks all at once. He made folks sort of in His spare time. For instance, one day He had a little time on his hands, so He got the clay, seasoned it the way He wanted it, then He laid it by and went on to doing something more important. Another day He had some spare moments, so He rolled it all out, and cut out the human shapes, and stood them all up against His long gold fence to dry while He did some important creating. The human shapes all got dry, and when He found time, He blowed the breath of life in them. After that, from time to time, He would call everybody up, and give them spare parts.

For instance, one day He called everybody and gave out feet and eyes. Another time, He give out toe-nails that

Old Maker figured they could use. Anyhow, they had all that they got up to now. So then one day He said, 'Tomorrow morning, at seven o'clock sharp, *I aim to give out color.* Everybody *be here on time. I got plenty of creating to do tomorrow, and I want to give out this color and get it over wid. Everybody be 'round de throne at seven o' clock tomorrow morning!'*

So next morning at seven o'clock, God was sitting on His throne with His big crown on His head and seven suns circling around His head. Great multitudes was standing around the throne waiting to get their color. God sat up there and looked east, and He looked west, and He looked north and. . .He looked over to His left and moved His hands over a crowd and said, 'You's yellow people!' They all bowed low and said, 'Thank you, God,' and they went on off. He looked at another crowd, moved His hands over them and said, 'You's red folks!' They made their manners and said, 'Thank you, Old Maker,' and they went on off. He looked towards the center and moved His hands over another crowd and said, 'You's white folks!' They bowed low and said, 'Much obliged, Jesus,' and they went on off. Then God looked way over to the right and said, 'Look here, Gabriel, I miss a lot of multitudes from around the throne this morning.' Gabriel looked too, and said, 'Yessir, there's a heap of multitudes missing from round de throne this morning.' So God sat there an hour and a half and waited. Then He called Gabriel and said, 'Looka here, Gabriel, I'm sick and tired of this waiting. I got plenty of creating to do this morning. You go find them folks and tell 'em they better hurry on up here if they expect to get any color. Fool with me, and I won't give out no more.'

So Gabriel run on off and started hunting around. Way

after while, he found the missing multitudes lying around on the grass by the Sea of Life, fast asleep. So Gabriel woke them up and told them, 'You better get up from there and come on up to the throne and get your color. Old Maker is might wore out from waiting. Fool with Him and He won't give out no more color.'

So as the multitudes heard that, they all jumped up and went running towards the throne hollering, 'Give us our color! We want our color! We got just as much right to color as anybody else.' So when the first ones got to the throne, they tried to stop and be polite. But the ones coming on behind got to pushing and shoving so till the first ones got shoved all up against the throne...till the throne was careening all over to one side. So God said, 'Here! Here! Git back! Git back!' But they was keeping up such a racket that they misunderstood Him, and thought He said, 'Git black!' So they just got black, and kept the thing a-going.

That was the way Zora had always heard it, and she wondered how people had become so confused over the years. Why did they act like color was either a blessing or a curse? Couldn't they see it had always been a gift?

4

Mama

When Zora was 13, her mother got sick. Lucy Hurston had always been rather frail, but she had such a strong spirit, people didn't usually notice how small and delicate she was. She had just come home from her sister's funeral in Alabama, and she seemed distant and tired. But Zora wasn't worried. She knew her mother would recover.

Mama needed more help around the house once she got sick. It took her a long time to finish even one of the many tasks she had always done every day. Supper came later and later, and the house wasn't as clean anymore. Mama and Papa seemed to have troubles between them, too. At night, from her bed, Zora could hear them arguing, their angry voices rising and falling. Until she got sick, Mama usually won the arguments. She just kept on disagreeing with Papa until he shut up or slammed out of the house. But now her voice sounded strained and frantic. And Papa would continue yelling long after Mama had grown completely silent.

After a few weeks, Mama got so weak she stayed in bed most of the time. Her small body almost disappeared into the feather mattress, and her smooth, dusky skin developed a yellow cast to it, like the brass headboard only dull, Zora thought. Then women from town took turns bringing food over so Papa and the children could eat. But Zora thought these things were only temporary.

One afternoon, when Zora was sitting out in the yard, Sarah came to say Mama wanted to talk to her. So Zora got up and went on in. She stood in the doorway for a few moments because she wasn't sure Mama was still awake. But then Mama saw her and motioned her over to the bed.

"Hello, baby. I just want to tell you a few things. Sit down here on the side of the bed." Zora walked over and sat on the edge of the mattress. Mama smiled at her and started talking again. "You know we all got to die one day," she said, "and my day will be coming. I just want you to do some things for me. Will you listen to me, baby?"

Zora was surprised that her mother wanted to talk about death in the middle of the day. Maybe her fever was making her feel confused. But Zora kept these thoughts to herself. Instead she smiled. "Yes, Mama," she answered.

"Now when my time comes, don't let them take the pillow from under my head. I know it's the village custom, but I don't want it."

Zora nodded. The townspeople believed that removing the pillow from a dying person's head eased their suffering.

"And don't let nobody cover the mirror or the clock, neither. I don't want it. You understand me, Zora?"

Again Zora nodded her head. At death, all clocks and mirrors were covered with cloth so the departing spirit wouldn't damage them in any way. Zora looked into her mother's eyes, which shone like bottomless dark pools. She noticed her mother was breathing more heavily than usual. It hurt her to see Mama so helpless. And it was strange to be sitting beside her this way. Usually it was Mama stroking Zora's forehead when she was sick. Or Mama sitting in the corner rocker with her sewing, humming some sad old song. It was Mama taking care of *her*. Now, it seemed,

Mama was a motherless child.

"It's okay, baby." Mama's voice startled Zora. It sounded hoarse and weak. "You go on back outside and play some more." Mama stretched her fingers across the sheet to the place where Zora's arm was resting and brushed her fingertips against Zora's skin. They felt cool and dry. "Go on back outside, Zora." And Mama smiled a little.

Later, in the evening, as Zora sat on the gate-post, she saw her father come walking slowly down the road toward the house. He passed her without speaking and went inside. A few minutes later, Zora's brother Joel came out of the house and headed down the road toward the store. Zora watched his shape shrink as he moved into the distance. Everything seemed to be happening so much more slowly than usual. It was as though the world, instead of spinning on its axis, were slowly winding down to a stop. And the sky seemed swollen, like a dense liquid overhead that made it harder to breathe. Zora felt lonely. Usually this time of day was her favorite, with Mama cooking and all the kids arguing or playing in the yard. Now it was quiet, an aching quiet.

An awful feeling started traveling across Zora's skin, and she couldn't shake it. She felt as though she were about to remember something — something momentous — but she didn't know what it was. After a while, she saw Sally Bailey and Mary Mosely and Cally Johnson's mama coming down the road. They nodded at her when they reached the gate, then went inside her house. A few minutes later two more women arrived and went inside. Then Joel came trotting toward her and ran inside the house without stopping. Something was going on. Zora slid off the fence and went inside to see.

They were all in Mama's room, and Mama had her head twisted back on the pillow, the sheets tangled around her fingers, and was breathing loudly. Nobody looked up when Zora walked in. They were all staring at Mama's small face. Papa was leaning against the washstand with his head down. He seemed more like a boy than the powerful man he was. Zora moved slowly toward the foot of the bed. She felt frightened, but she didn't understand what was scaring her so much. She could hardly bear to look at her mother because she seemed to be suffering so. But at the same time, she couldn't look anywhere else.

As a grown woman, looking back on that time, Zora wrote:

The Master-Maker in His making had made Old Death. Made him with big, soft feet and square toes. Made him with a face that reflects the face of all things, but neither changes itself, nor is mirrored anywhere. Made the body of Death out of infinite hunger. Made a weapon for his hand to satisfy his needs. This was the morning of the day of the beginning of things.

But Death had no home and he knew it at once.

"And where shall I dwell in my dwelling?" Old Death asked, for he was already old when he was made.

"You shall build you a place close to the living, yet far out of the sight of eyes. Wherever there is a building, there you have your platform that comprehends the four roads of the winds. For your hunger, I give you the first and last taste of all things."

We had been born, so Death had had his first taste of us. We had built things, so he had his platform in our yard.

And now, Death stirred from his platform in his secret place in our yard, and came inside the house.

Mama's breathing grew so loud it seemed deafening, and one of the women in the room finally spoke. "I think it's time we took the pillow." Mrs. Johnson reached her hand toward the bed, but Zora lunged forward to stop it.

"No! No! Don't touch it! She said to leave it!" Zora could hear her own heart pounding so hard, it sounded like it had jumped inside her head. And the air in the room felt thick and heavy. She struggled to force her way through it to the head of the bed, but Papa grabbed her and pulled her back.

"No, Papa, no! She doesn't want—"

"Shut-up that yelling!" Papa's voice was gruff. "Can't you see your Mama's dying?"

Zora jerked her body forward, trying to escape his grasp, but he was too strong. Mrs. Johnson eased the pillow out from under Mama's head and held it in her lap. Zora started crying, so hard she could barely see, but she could feel a roomful of stares directed her way.

"Best cover up the clock, too, and the mirror."

"No! Don't do it!" But Zora felt her strength fading. Mama didn't even seem aware that anyone was in the room with her. She was just struggling to breathe, although her chest hardly seemed to move. Zora buried her face in Papa's side and cried harder. When she finally stopped, the room was silent. Mama was dead.

That evening, the village of Eatonville gathered at the Hurston house and stood in the yard talking in low voices. That was the way people comforted each other in time of death. Bob was on his way home from boarding school in Jacksonville. When he finally arrived and saw all the people in his yard, he knew at once that his mother was dead.

The next day they buried Mama, and that night Zora and her brothers and sister gathered around the organ and mourned their loss. When Papa came in, he joined them, and cried like a bewildered child. The house felt strange, like some other family belonged there besides this grieving crowd. Zora kept looking toward the kitchen, expecting to see Mama come walking in with a plate of cookies, but she didn't. Mama was gone. And though none of the children realized it that night, it would be the last time they all gathered in the house together.

The next day, Bob went back to Jacksonville to school, and Sarah with him. And since Papa was hardly ever home anymore, because of his preaching and other work, he soon decided to send Zora to board there, too. She was really too young for the school, but under the circumstances special arrangements were made. Since Sarah would be there, she was to help look after Zora.

So two weeks after her mother died, Zora left home. Her brother Dick took her to catch the train to Jacksonville. Their sadness seemed to fill the bags and spill over into the back of the wagon as they drove through the star-filled Florida night. Zora had always known she would leave Eatonville one day. But she had never imagined she would leave in the midst of so much sorrow and regret. Her mother had asked her — Zora — to do those simple things for her at her death, and Zora had failed. And she would never be able to tell Mama how sorry she was. Mama had put her trust in Zora. Now Zora was hunched over in a battered wagon, with a heavy heart, headed toward an uncertain destiny.

5

Jacksonville

The first thing Zora noticed about Jacksonville was the way white people treated her. In Maitland, she had grown used to their easy smiles on the street. Whenever she went in any store, whether it was Joe Clarke's in Eatonville or one of the white shops of Maitland, she had always been greeted with a happy hello and a piece of candy or a little bag of crackers. But in Jacksonville white people were different. They said hello to each other, but whenever they encountered a black person they were silent. Zora began to feel invisible. And their stern, pinched faces frightened her a little.

The school she attended was a black school, so she didn't have to worry about white folks there. Zora liked her classes, too, except for arithmetic — which is called math now. She never could understand the point of putting numbers together and then taking them apart again in different ways. And she could have lived without the food they served at the school. Breakfast every day was grits and gravy, but she got used to it. She never liked it, but she got used to it.

The worst thing about Jacksonville was the loneliness. She missed the woods at home, which were full of squirrels and birds and tiny blossoms. She missed the call of owls at night. She missed her house, the yard full of trees and the

way the moon drifted across the sky at night. She missed her other brothers. But more than anything, she missed her mother. At night as she lay in bed trying to sleep, she felt an aching sadness balloon inside her. And some mornings she leapt out of bed and started to run into the kitchen to Mama before she remembered she was away from home, in Jacksonville, and that her mother was dead.

Sometimes her teachers would line the girls up in pairs and take them out to sightsee in town. One day, as Zora stood in one of these lines near a street corner, she looked across the road to a large, shuttered house. A woman sat on the porch in a rocker, sewing quietly. She looked like Mama. Maybe she was Mama! Maybe she hadn't died at all, but just moved to Jacksonville! Zora grew so excited, she was ready to break out of the line and run across the street. But then the woman stood up, brushed off the front of her dress, and went inside the house. Zora felt tears wetting the corners of her eyes. The woman was tall, not short like Mama.

Since she was the youngest girl at the school, it was hard to make friends. The others, who were at least two years older, didn't want to be bothered. Whenever Zora entered a room where they sat giggling and whispering their secrets, the room immediately became silent. Then they would tell her to go away, to go fix her hair or her dress. They said she was too little to understand what they were talking about.

And Sarah grew sadder and quieter and more withdrawn every day. She missed home, too, especially Papa, since they had always been close. From the time Sarah was born, he had babied and spoiled her. He couldn't stand for her to feel the smallest unhappiness. So when Papa found out that Sarah was miserable at school, he sent for her, and Zora felt completely alone. Even though Bob was at the same school, he was so much older she hardly saw him.

She tried to concentrate on her studies. There were a few good things she had discovered at the school. She liked writing notes during chapel ceremonies. And she had discovered a way to sneak through the fence to the store across the street, where she bought gingersnaps and pickles with the few cents she had. And when the city of Jacksonville held a spelling bee for all the black schools, Zora won it for hers. She was given a world atlas and a Bible, plus all the lemonade and cake she could hold. And all the teachers kept congratulating her and telling her how proud they were. That was nice. She started feeling a little like a star.

One day, a few weeks after Sarah left, Zora got a letter from her. It said that Papa had remarried. Zora read the awful words over and over, trying to believe them. Mama hadn't been dead three months, and Papa had married another woman! Zora had a stepmother! And the first thing this stepmother had done was order Papa to make Sarah leave the house! As she read the news, Zora could feel her face burn with anger and with pain. How could Papa do such a thing? Hadn't he loved Mama? And how could he drive his own daughter out of her home? If he had done it to Zora, it wouldn't have been so disgraceful. Zora knew he had never been overly fond of her. But Papa had been Sarah's whole world!

So Zora stayed at school alone. Her teachers seemed to like her a lot. She could always be counted on for the correct answers to questions. Her tendency to talk back bothered them a little, but her brains made up for it. Little by little, she began to adjust to life in Jacksonville. She wasn't actually happy. Jacksonville seemed dim compared to the bright sunshine of Eatonville. But it was alright.

One day one of the directors of the school called Zora into her office and closed the door. She said Zora's tuition and board had not been paid in several months, and she wanted to know what Zora intended to do about it. Zora just shrugged her shoulders. How did she know? Papa was the one who was supposed to take care of that. So the director let her go.

But a few days later, she called Zora in again and asked her the same question. Again Zora said she didn't know what to do. So the director let her go again. This continued for several weeks, except that, after a while, the director no longer bothered to close the door to her office. Then she started confronting Zora in the hallway. Once she even yelled her question out the window to the schoolyard below, where Zora was playing at the time.

Zora began to dread these encounters. They made her feel ashamed, and that was a new feeling, one she didn't like. Sometimes she caught herself ducking her head when she passed grownups in the hallway. And when her schoolmates stared at her, she wanted to shrink to a dot and disappear; she wanted to be invisible.

Finally, the director quit bothering Zora with her questions. Instead she put her to work. After classes, Zora had to scrub stairs or help in the kitchen or mop floors. But work was a thousand times better than the awful shame she had felt before.

When the end of the school year came, Bob left to take a job. He said Papa would come for Zora in a few days, so she stayed behind. But days passed, then weeks, and there was no Papa. Zora grew tired of gazing out the window at the school's front walk, looking for Papa's tall figure to come loping down it. Every day was just like the day before, only emptier. But finally word came. The director called Zora into her office to read Papa's letter.

It said he wasn't coming, and it offered to let the school adopt her. After Zora read it, it took her several moments to become conscious of her surroundings again. She felt like she had just broken into a million tiny pieces, as if the particles that had once made up the body of Zora Hurston were floating around the room like dust. The sunlight felt raw and unfriendly. A wave of nausea hit her stomach.

"We are not in the position to adopt any children," the director was saying, only her voice was a little softer than usual. It almost sounded kind. "I'm going to have to send you home. When you get there, tell your father to send me the money for your fare." She reached down into the bottom of her bag and handed Zora a dollar and a half.

The next day, Zora boarded a steamboat for the trip down the St. John's River to Sanford. She stood on a lower deck as the boat pulled out, watching the crowd of people waving from the dock. There was nobody waving goodbye to her. A little further down the river, the shores began to brighten until they became a rush of green, and Zora's spirits rose. Trees! How good it felt to see forests again! Occasionally an alligator's bumpy body would slide off a rock into the water and swim away from the boat. Birds rose from the surface then drifted down again when it was safe. Schools of fish passed alongside the boat. Some of the catfish were as long as men. Zora began to relax. She hadn't realized how tight and tense she had grown in Jacksonville.

The boat itself was beautiful, full of red carpeting and

shiny brass railings. In some of the big rooms on board, chandeliers threw splintered reflections across the floor. Zora watched white-jacketed waiters rush in and out of the dining room; the clink of dishes lasted all day and into the night. One of the waiters brought her some fried chicken and a big slice of pie and made her go to the back of the boat to eat it. There she watched a circle of black workmen in blue overalls hunch near the railing to eat their lunches out of shoe boxes.

The next day the boat docked in Sanford, and Zora walked to the rail station to catch the train to Maitland. When she climbed on board, she recognized the porter. It was the same porter who had laughed when she'd tried to escape her first train ride. He smiled and nodded at her, but made no mention of that day so many years before. She was glad. She took a seat by the window and watched the countryside rush up to meet her. In less than an hour, she would be home again.

6

The Feather Mattress

But Jacksonville had given her only a small taste of the hardships that lay ahead. When she walked through the gate to her family's house in Eatonville, Zora could tell that a world of change had taken place. The house still looked the same, but it had a feel that was not at all friendly. Sarah and three older brothers no longer lived there. Nor did Everett, the baby; Sarah had married and taken him with her. So there were only Dick and Ben left at home, and now Zora.

But that wasn't what made the place seem different. There was a lingering sadness, a drab loneliness about it. And, of course, there was Zora's stepmother, who had no affection at all for Papa's children. It was clear that she wanted them all gone, the sooner the better. She cooked, but never on schedule. And she never washed any of their clothes — except Papa's — unless she felt like it, which wasn't often. But the thing that upset Zora the most was the way she acted as though the house had always belonged to her. Take Mama's feather mattress, for instance. It made Zora sick to see her stepmother propped up in bed like some queen. Mama had brought that mattress from her father's house when she married Papa. What right did this imposter have to it? The more Zora thought about the injustice, the angrier she got. So it was only a matter of time before trouble erupted. In less than a week, Zora reached her limit.

She decided to take the mattress away from her stepmother, and she went round to where her brother John lived and told him about her plans. She knew she was going to need some help defending herself. All the next afternoon, Zora sat on the gate-post staring down the road looking for John. When at last she saw his lanky figure headed toward the house, she ran inside and pulled the mattress off the bed. She had dragged it all the way into the yard before her stepmother noticed and started screaming for Papa. She looked mad enough to spit fire.

When Papa appeared out of nowhere and started running for Zora with his fist out, John stepped around the chinaberry tree and moved between them. "Leave her alone, Papa," he said. "You know this is Mama's mattress."

But Papa didn't stop moving. He just changed direction and aimed for John, reaching into his back pocket at the same time. "You best get out of here!" he growled at his son. Then Zora saw the flash of a knife blade in Papa's hand.

John had seen it, too, but stood his ground, and father and son stood face to face for a long time without saying a word. Zora was gripping the edge of the mattress so hard her hand was going numb. She was afraid of what Papa might do. She had never seen him so angry — to pull a knife on his own flesh and blood! But finally he lowered his arm and turned back toward the house. Then he went inside with his head down, without even looking at his wife.

Zora and John turned away and carried the mattress between them out of the yard and down the road to town. For the longest time, they could hear their stepmother's voice screeching across the distance.

Having no home, Zora went to live with relatives. When they got tired of her, she went to live with different relatives, then with some friends of her mother's. Nobody could understand her attitude. Why didn't she act the least bit grateful for their charity? Didn't she realize she was penniless, parentless? Here they were giving her food to eat and a place to sleep, and all she could do was mope around. They couldn't understand this child at all.

But the real problem wasn't her attitude; it was poverty. In Eatonville, when her mother was still alive, Zora had never wanted for anything. She had plenty of food to eat and enough clothes to keep her comfortable. She had a home and friends. Since everyone in town was black, she had not known racism. She had attended school regularly, thanks to her mother, and developed a love of reading and language that would last the rest of her life. So when she left Eatonville and entered a world full of hatred and poverty, it seemed so alien and unfriendly that, for a while, she thought she would never recover. As she described it later: "There is something about poverty that smells like death. Dead dreams dropping off the heart like leaves in a dry season and rotting around the feet....People can be slave ships in shoes."

It was impossible for Zora to explain her feelings to the people around her. At the time, she could hardly understand them herself. She had so many things bottled up inside — anger, sadness, fear, longing. She was angry because she didn't have a home, because her father didn't care, never had. She was sad because she missed her mother and the rest of her family. She was afraid because she didn't know what was going to happen to her. And she longed for books to read, for a quiet place to daydream again, for a place where she felt loved.

Every family she lived with, sooner or later, started

urging her to find a job. Sometimes they let her go to school for a while first, and then she was happy — except she knew it would never last. Sure enough, in a few weeks, they'd pull her out of class and tell her she needed to get a job. She'd try to explain how important school was, but they wouldn't listen.

"That's real nice, honey," they'd say, "but there's a housekeeping job over in town that pays a dollar a week. Food ain't free, you know."

So Zora would go ask for the job, only to be told she was too young. Then she would go from door to door, asking for work. Since she was small for her age, most people turned her away as soon as they saw her. But every once in a while, someone would hire her.

For the next few years, she survived this way. Most of the jobs she got lasted only a few days or weeks. Her heart just wasn't in them. She wanted to be out learning and exploring, not cleaning people's kitchens or taking care of their kids. Eventually she landed a job as a doctor's helper, and then she got a letter from her brother Bob. He wanted her to come live with him and his wife and children. He wanted to help her go back to school. He sent her the train fare and said for her to come at once. Zora was elated. Years later she could still recall the feelings the letter and the train ride aroused in her. She wrote: "It was near night. I shall never forget how the red ball of the sun hung on the horizon and raced along with the train for a short space, and then plunged below the belly-band of the earth. There have been other suns that set in significance for me, but *that* sun!...I remember the long, strung-out cloud that measured it for the fall."

7

Friends

When Zora got to her brother's house and met his wife and three children, she began to relax for the first time in months. It was good to be with family again, to feel the comfort of kinship.

After supper the first night, Bob asked her to go for a walk with him, and he told her he wasn't prepared to send her to school just yet. He wanted her to help out with the children and the house a while, then he would see what he could do.

Zora felt sick. Ever since Bob sent for her she had been numb with excitement at the thought of going to high school. For the first time, the awful staleness of the years since Mama's death had seemed to lift off her shoulders — and now this. But she kept her disappointment to herself; she didn't want her brother to be sorry he had asked her to come.

The next morning Bob woke her at dawn and asked her to go downstairs and start a fire. But he warned her to be quiet; he didn't want to wake his wife. The next day he asked Zora to make breakfast, too, and clean up around the kitchen. And every day after that he added another job or two to the list. He said he wanted his wife to be happy, that she deserved some help after everything she had done for him and the children. Zora didn't say anything, but something about his attitude didn't seem right.

She liked the children, though. When she finished her work in the afternoons, she played with them and told them stories. Then she felt like a small child again herself, and forgot the emptiness that nagged her the rest of the day.

Weeks passed, then months, and there was still no sign of school in Zora's future. As time wore on, she started feeling less like a member of her brother's family and more like his maid. It seemed that she was always working. She had no friends of her own, and little privacy. The only times she felt the least bit happy, besides the afternoons with the children, were when her sister-in-law sent her out of the house on an errand. Then she would dawdle, taking a long time to complete her mission, pretending to be free again.

One afternoon, on a trip to the market, Zora lapsed so deeply into a daydream she forgot where she was and what she was there for. As she drifted around a corner, she bumped into a tall white woman. The force of the impact knocked the woman's groceries out of her arms and jolted Zora out of her fantasy.

"Oh! I'm sorry!" she exclaimed, and quickly bent to pick up the fallen items. When she looked up, the woman was smiling at her.

"What's your name?" she asked, so Zora told her.

"You look about the same age as my daughter," the woman said, and then a pale, black-haired girl a little taller than Zora walked up.

"Valena, this is Zora. She's been nice enough to help me with my groceries. Maybe she'd like to come by the house and have some lemonade with us." The woman looked at Zora. Zora hesitated a moment, then nodded.

"Yes, ma'am. Thank you. I'm real sorry for bumping

into you." But the woman waved her apology away with a flick of the wrist.

After that, Zora visited Valena and her mother whenever she could get away. But she didn't tell her brother about the friendship because she was afraid he would forbid it. It had been so long since anyone had treated her kindly, even the smallest gestures were precious, and she guarded her new friendship carefully.

One afternoon, while she was dusting the china cabinet in her brother's front room, she heard somebody whistling outside. So she peeked through the draperies to see who it was. Valena's brother was standing on the opposite corner. When he saw her face, he motioned for her to come outside. Without hesitating, Zora hurried out the front door and across the street.

"My mother wants you," was all the boy said before running off down the sidewalk.

When Zora got to Valena's house, everything was in an uproar.

"Oh, Zora! There you are! We found you a job! Quick, go wash up and put on this dress." Valena held up a new blue dress with a tiny white collar. Zora was dumbfounded.

"Hurry up, Zora! The lady's waiting!" Zora stared at their urgent faces for a few moments, then hurriedly started changing clothes. Valena's father had discovered that one of the actors performing at the theatre downtown needed a new maid. Whoever the woman hired would have to travel with her, since the show was due to move to the next town at the end of the week. Zora washed her face and hands and nervously combed her hair. Valena loaned her a hat and helped polish her shoes. Then Zora set off for the theatre.

When she got there, the dressing rooms were all empty.

She had been told to knock on the third door, but it stood ajar, so she waited restlessly in the hallway. From some other room, she could hear a high sweet voice singing. When it stopped, a young blond woman about 20 came down the hall, went into the third room, and closed the door. Zora hesitated a few minutes, then knocked softly.

"Come in!" the sweet voice called. Zora opened the door and walked in. The blond woman sat at her dressing table. She examined Zora in the mirror first, then turned around. "Who are you?"

"I'm Zora. I came to work for you." To her surprise, the blond woman threw back her head and laughed. Then she looked Zora over from top to bottom.

"But you're just a child! How old are you?"

"Twenty," Zora lied. Again the young woman laughed.

"No, really, how old?"

"Eighteen." But this time, when the woman laughed, Zora laughed too. "Sixteen?" she asked, but it didn't matter. Zora liked this woman already.

"Okay, we'll stop there. You can have the job. Let's not bring up the subject of age again, though, to be safe." Then the woman winked at Zora and giggled to herself as she finished up at the dressing table.

Zora was so excited, she was afraid to go back to her brother's house at all. She was afraid he wouldn't let her leave again. All he seemed to care about was having someone to do his wife's work for her. So all that week Zora slept on a cot beside Valena's bed. They were both so excited about Zora's new job, they stayed up talking most of the night. And that week the blond woman — Zora called her Miss M — let Zora stand backstage and watch her sing. At the end of the week, she gave Zora money to buy a suitcase for her new life on the road. Since Zora had only one nice dress to put in it, she stuffed the suitcase with newspaper so her comb and other toiletries wouldn't rattle around inside. She didn't want Miss M to know just how poor she was.

Zora was the only black person traveling with the acting company, but it didn't matter. She got along with all the actors. In fact, they were always competing for Zora's attention. They liked to hear her talk and were always thinking up ways to tease her into calling them names. Zora realized later that, since they had all grown up in the North, they weren't used to hearing a Southern child talk. She explained: "They did not know of the way an average Southern child, white or black, is raised.... It is an everyday affair to hear somebody called a mullet-headed, mule-eared, wall-eyed, hog-nosed, 'gator-faced, shad-mouthed, screw-necked, goat-bellied, puzzle-gutted, camel-backed, butt-sprung, battle-hammed, knock-kneed, razor-legged, box-ankled, shovel-footed, unmated so-and-so!"

Zora stayed with the company for a year and a half. The actors made her feel happy and loved for the first time in years. They bought her ice cream sundaes and Coca Colas and exchanged notes and sang their songs for her. They introduced her to the world. Before, she had known only Eatonville, Jacksonville and a handful of little towns around south central Florida. With the company she traveled out of the state for the first time. And they told her about places called New York and Philadelphia and Paris. She hadn't realized the world held so much between Eatonville and the horizon. So it was with lighter spirits that she left the company in Baltimore, Maryland, determined to finish school and make something of her life.

8

High School

But it wasn't long before she ran out of money. It went fast. With the acting company, Zora had always been able to count on meals and a place to sleep, but in Baltimore, she had to provide everything for herself, and she simply did not have enough money.

On top of that, the city frightened her a little. She had never been around so many people and felt so alone. And she missed the Florida countryside. In Baltimore there were only cold stone buildings and shipyards. Even the ocean seemed indifferent, huge and steely grey.

She got a job as a waitress and might have been a good one if her heart had been in the job. But she hated the way the customers treated her, as though she were their personal servant. Then she got sick and had to have her appendix removed. Despite the hardships, however, she remained determined to go to school. As soon as she could she enrolled at the city's night high school. She was going to get an education — money or no money.

School made life brighter and more bearable. Zora still worked most of the day at low-paying jobs, but her night classes made up for the drudgery. Her favorite was English, mostly because of the teacher, Dwight Holmes, a young black man. He didn't have to say anything directly, but the way he looked at Zora made her feel hopeful about the future. He made her want to explore again, as though the world were a magnificent and wondrous thing. When he read aloud to the class, Zora leaned back and listened, and his voice called up magical images in her mind.

One night he read a poem called "Kubla Khan." It seemed to Zora that he was reading it just for her. As he pronounced the words, she felt them float across the room to her. And when he looked up from the page, she knew it was straight into her eyes. When he finished and dismissed the class, it took several moments for Zora to recover enough to stand up. When she did, Mr. Holmes walked over to her desk.

"Miss Hurston?" he said softly. "I just wanted to tell you what good work you've been doing. Keep it up." Then he turned and walked back to his desk at the front of the room.

Zora was so happy she was unaware of the traffic on the streets as she walked home. In fact, it seemed that she moved out of the school and into her room in one step. Something told her she was on the right track again — she would get to the horizon yet. And she made up her mind to study harder. She went back to the night high school a few more times, then switched to the high school program at Morgan College. It didn't seem to matter that she owned only one dress, one change of underwear and a single pair of shoes. Or that her classmates soon began teasing her about wearing the same clothes every day. She didn't really care. She realized the only way out of the bleak hole she had fallen into after Mama's death was through education. If she could just hang on long enough, things were bound to change.

9

Washington, D.C.

By sheer will power, Zora managed to survive the next few years. As before, she moved from job to job, struggling to make a living. In the early 1900s, it was unusual for a young unmarried woman to be on her own in a big city like Baltimore. And since Zora was a young black woman, the odds were stacked against her. But she grew used to the blank stares of white people. After a while she learned to block them out of her mind completely most of the time. She began to make friends with the other young women at Morgan College, a black school, though most of them came from middle class or wealthy families. Because she was bright and eager to learn, both her teachers and her classmates paid her extra attention. Little by little, she began to make up for the years of school she had missed, and chipped away at a high school education. Eventually she even began to think of college.

When someone suggested she go to Howard University, Zora was shocked. It was the best black college in the country! Howard was to blacks what Harvard was to whites, and to imagine herself in its prestigious hallways was almost impossible — at first. Gradually, however, she came to like the idea. She remembered what her mother had always said: "jump at de sun!" She had to believe in herself. If she didn't, who would?

So she left Baltimore and headed for Washington, D.C., and Howard University. At the time, in 1918, World War I was coming to a close, and Washington was still reeling from it. Thousands of people had flooded the city to help direct the war effort. In little more than a year, more than 100,000 people had moved to the nation's capital. Zora was one of the last of these arrivals.

Washington has always had a large black population. Even today, most of its inhabitants are African Americans. Zora fit in easily and, for the first time since Eatonville, began to feel part of a larger community. She quickly found a job as a waitress, then landed a position as a manicurist in a downtown barbershop not far from the White House. The barbershop was run by a black man named George Robinson, who owned several other shops as well, but most of them, including the one Zora worked in, served only white customers.

That was because of a practice called segregation. This practice, common across the southern United States and reaching even into the nation's capital, was designed to keep blacks and whites separate. There were schools, restaurants and shops for whites and another set for blacks. There were even laws to make sure things stayed separate; they were called "Jim Crow" laws.

Many people claimed the Jim Crow system was fair. They called it "separate but equal." But the truth is that white schools and public facilities were given much more money to operate, while their black counterparts got practically none. White teachers got paid more. White schoolchildren rode buses to school. Black schools were overcrowded, rundown, sometimes even lacking heat in the winter. And many black children had to walk several miles each day to school and back.

In some southern states, the laws were extreme. Some required that blacks and whites use separate telephone booths, and that the courts use separate Bibles to swear in black witnesses. Blacks were excluded from most white hotels and apartment buildings unless they worked there. Then they had to enter through special doorways and use separate staircases.

Since the barbershop where Zora worked was near so many government offices, most of its customers were politicians or news men. Zora worked from 3:30 to 8:30 every evening, and found herself in the company of senators, congressmen, bankers, news reporters and members of the Cabinet. Most of them treated her kindly. A few even paid her extra attention, taking time to discuss politics with her or to talk about life in general. Sometimes she heard news from her customers days before it appeared in the papers. It wasn't that the politicians trusted her more than anyone else. (Zora didn't fool herself by believing that.) Even if she were to tell someone what she'd heard, she would never have been believed. She knew no one would take the word of a young black manicurist about the affairs of Washington's powerful white senators.

By working through the summer, she managed to save enough money to enroll for the first quarter of classes at Howard University. It was hard balancing college and a job. When she finished her classes each day, she had to go right to work, and when she got off work, there were assignments to do. During the seven years that Zora lived in Washington, she finished a year and half of college. She also held down her job as a manicurist, and served at times as a maid for wealthy black families in the city. If she hadn't had to support herself, she might have finished college in those seven years. But in many ways, her jobs were just as educational as Howard University.

Day after day in the barbershop, she listened to stories of goings-on in the White House and Congress. She met men who had traveled the world, and sometimes they took the time to tell her about what they had seen. One congressman even helped her with especially difficult assignments from school.

Even though all the people who worked in the barbershop were black and all the customers rich and powerful white men, Zora never worried too much about it. She got along fine with them all. But one afternoon a black man walked into the shop from the street and plopped down in one of the barber chairs. "I'd like a haircut," he said.

At first everyone just stared at him. Couldn't the stranger see this shop was for *whites*? All he had to do was look around. Finally, the manager walked over to him.

"Excuse me, sir, but you'll have to leave. This shop serves whites only. There's a colored shop way up on U Street. You can get your hair cut there."

"No. I want a haircut in *this* shop." The man crossed his arms and leaned stubbornly back in the chair.

The manager shifted his feet. It was clear he was getting more frustrated by the minute. "Didn't you hear what I said? We can't serve you here. Now get up and get out!" With that he lifted the intruder by the arm and escorted him toward the door. But the minute he let go, the man plopped down in another barber chair and refused to budge.

"It's my right to get a haircut in this shop, and that's what I want." It was obvious he intended to stay as long as it took. But almost in unison, several of the barbers and

porters and a few customers rose to chase the man out. Two of the largest barbers dragged him out into the street and dropped him, where he remained until a car came along. Then he jumped up and ran away down the sidewalk. Everyone relaxed a little and went back to their business.

That night, as Zora lay in bed, she thought about the incident. The stranger had been right: he should have been able to get a haircut in any shop. It was wrong to exclude a person just because of the color of his skin. But if the manager had given in and cut the man's hair, all the white customers would have walked out and taken their business elsewhere. Then Mr. Robinson, the owner of the shop, who was a very nice man who went out of his way to help black people whenever he could, would have gone out of business. And Zora and the other employees would have been out of jobs. Was that what the stranger wanted to happen? Zora didn't think so, but it was unsettling to realize the way things really worked. Even though Zora and the other barbershop employees were black like the man from the street, their first concern had been taking care of themselves — not helping a black brother get treated fairly.

Zora had always been popular in school, mainly because of her sense of humor and ability to tell a good story. In Eatonville, after all, she had grown up among some of the best storytellers of the age. But at Howard University, a new world began opening its doors to her — the world of writing. It was similar to talking on the store porch. But where the talker uses her voice to convey a feeling, the writer uses carefully chosen words.

Zora had always impressed her English teachers with her enthusiasm and talent. So it was no surprise when she proved to be a good writer, too. Soon she was invited to join the Stylus, a campus club open only to students with the ability to write well. Shortly after joining the club, Zora published her first short story in the club's newspaper.

One of the club's sponsors was a man named Alain Locke, who taught philosophy at Howard University. He was a brilliant man — a Harvard graduate and Rhodes Scholar — who took a personal interest in Zora and several other talented students.

Soon Zora received a letter from another influential man, Charles S. Johnson, who lived in New York City and published a magazine called *Opportunity.* He had read Zora's story. He was writing to black college students across the country asking for stories, poems or plays to publish in his magazine. He was also sponsoring a contest. Zora sent him another story and a play. Both won second place awards. In Johnson's next letter he mentioned New York City. That started Zora thinking about a permanent move North.

10

Harlem

Between 1910 and 1920, the United States changed in many ways. The Boy Scouts of America were founded. Arizona and New Mexico became states. Airplanes flew across the Atlantic Ocean for the first time. And black men and women began to move from southern farms to northern cities.

They headed north for several reasons. For one thing, new machines began to make farming easier, so it required fewer people. And new jobs were opening up in cities, primarily in factories. So black men and women used the opportunity to escape the hard physical labor of the rural South. Most believed they were moving to a friendlier place, that they were escaping from poverty, prejudice and violence.

During this period more than one million blacks migrated north, so many that the movement is now called the Great Migration. One of the most popular destinations was New York City. But there was a city inside New York City that called them — Harlem.

A large neighborhood in the borough of Manhattan, Harlem first attracted black residents because of its affordable apartments and houses. Then it began drawing men and women from farther away: from the southern states, the West Indies and Africa. In 1925, when Zora arrived, it was crowded with people full of hope, energy and talent. Most had come from the South, and many had brought their music with them. At night they gathered in local clubs to play jazz and dance. It wasn't long before whites, excited by the new music, began traveling uptown each night to join them.

For the first time, large numbers of whites began to read books written by and about black men and women. Some of the most popular books were about Harlem itself. Soon they started inviting black artists to parties, teas and fancy balls. Unfortunately, all this enthusiasm did little lasting good. It did not eliminate prejudice or poverty. Black men were still beaten simply because they were black. And even some of Harlem's most famous artists still had to work long hours at low-paying jobs to survive.

When Zora arrived in New York City, she had $1.50 and "no job, no friends, and a lot of hope." So she headed for Charles Johnson's apartment. She didn't know anyone else.

Zora had lived in big cities before, but never one like New York. Perched on the edge of a busy harbor, it was brimming with people from around the world. Zora spent her first few days walking around trying to soak in the sights. On any street corner she might hear several different languages. Every block was awash with color. There were flowers and newsstands, ropes of laundry flapping in the breeze, fresh fish and poultry laid out on beds of ice, dark-eyed children giggling in doorways. And the clothes people wore! From flowing silk to the roughest burlap! By the end of the day her eyes ached from all the colors, shapes, shadows and movement she had seen on the streets.

If it weren't for Charles Johnson and his wife, Zora's

first weeks in the city would have been rough. But the Johnsons shared their meals with her, loaned her money to get around, and introduced her to people who could help her get established. The days went past at a dizzying rate, and Zora met more people faster than at any other time in her life.

Most evenings Zora's apartment was bustling with people — from jazz musicians to students. She owned no furniture at all when she first moved in, but within a matter of days her already wide circle of friends brought enough to fill the entire apartment comfortably. She cooked them a "hand chicken dinner" in appreciation. She called it a "hand" dinner because nobody remembered to bring the forks.

Many of her friends were writers. Countee Cullen and Langston Hughes were poets. And Arna Bontemps, Jessie Fauset and Wallace Thurman wrote fiction. Because black artists of all kinds became so popular and created so much, the period between 1919 and 1930 is called the Harlem Renaissance. It was a true rebirth of ideas and feelings getting expressed in boundless new ways. And Zora would become a central figure.

Everyone who visited her apartment was expected to bring a bit of food to add to the big pot she left on the stove. By the end of the evening, it produced enough stew to feed the crowd. Zora told stories, sang, played the harmonica, and impersonated people she had seen on the streets. Since she had a storyteller's ear for accents, she was a perfect mimic and quickly became the center of attention.

But sometimes she would get tired of the company and go off to another room to be alone. There she would sit in the dark with the door closed, listening to the laughter and conversation that echoed from her front rooms. Or she would pull out pencil and paper and begin to write. In a few minutes, she would forget anybody else was around. Bending over her table in the lamplight, she let the words of her imagination and memory flow together onto the page.

In May, Charles Johnson organized an awards dinner for the winners of the contest he had sponsored. Since she had won two second place prizes, Zora was one of the guests of honor. Because Johnson did a good job of spreading the word about the banquet, it was packed with famous and influential people, and Zora's talent and flair impressed them. Fannie Hurst, a well-known white author and one of the contest judges, liked Zora so much she immediately offered her a job as her private secretary. Later she discovered Zora could barely type and cared little for filing, but the two women remained close friends for years. Annie Nathan Meyer had something different to offer: a scholarship to Barnard College, the women's division of Columbia University.

11

“Papa” Franz

Zora started school in the fall. The scholarship she had been awarded made it possible for her to study without worrying too much about bills. Finally she had time to read long books, write more stories, and really think about things. Life had always been such a scramble. For the first time, she could pause and look back over it. And the future seemed a little easier, too.

At Barnard College, Zora was the only black student, but that fact never really bothered her. What made her nervous was the school's high reputation. Sometimes, when she walked down the corridors to class, she would stop and give her arm a pinch. To think back to Joe Clarke's store porch and the barefooted talkers, and then to look at the marble columns and gleaming floors of the college, was like glancing across two different planets. Surely one of them had to be a dream!

But it wasn't just Barnard College that made her feel that way. It had been a long time since she left Eatonville, and the further she wandered the more she wondered about her childhood. It seemed so different from anything she encountered in the North. In northern cities, especially, people seemed cut off from each other, even people of the same race. She thought of the stranger who demanded a haircut in Washington, D.C., how the black employees had dragged him out into the street. Nothing like that could have happenend in Eatonville. Hadn't her father and his friends been willing to risk their lives when they thought another black man was in danger?

But when she tried to explain her feelings to other people, and when she wrote about Eatonville in her stories, everyone acted as though the lives she described were purely make-believe. Then she met Franz Boas and things began to change.

Boas taught anthropology at Barnard College. When he came across a paper Zora had written for one of her classes, he was immediately impressed by its clear ideas and sparkling language. So he called Zora aside one day to talk about it. It was the beginning of a long, productive relationship.

Anthropologists study racial and cultural differences between people. From the start, Boas was fascinated by the things Zora told him about Eatonville, and he wanted to hear more. Like Zora, he knew the stories and songs of Eatonville were important, and he knew there was a danger they might disappear before anyone got a chance to write them down. After all, the country was changing rapidly. So he urged her to study folklore: the stories, songs, beliefs and customs people pass from generation to generation. And he pushed her hard and taught her how to discipline herself. "That man can make people work the hardest with just a look or word, than anyone else in creation," she wrote. "Get to the point is his idea....He wants facts, not guesses." But even though he was a tough taskmaster, his students loved him, especially Zora. They called him "Papa" Franz.

Zora worked hard at Barnard College. And she began to think of herself as a scientist instead of a writer. She liked working with facts and figures. Somehow they seemed so much cleaner and easier to understand than feelings and memories. One day, a few weeks before she was due to graduate from the college, Boas called her into his office and gave her some amazing news. He had arranged for her to go South and collect black folklore. When he asked where she wanted to go, she chose Florida. She knew the state was full of stories and songs. But there was another reason, too. "I realized that I was new myself," she wrote later, "so it looked sensible for me to choose familiar ground."

12

Home Folks

In 1927, when Zora headed south to collect folklore, not too many people had gone before. Hardly anyone had studied African-American folklore, and most of the few who had were white. There was only one other black folklorist in America who had as much training as Zora did. His name was Arthur Huff Fauset. But Zora had one advantage over him: she had grown up in the South, where most of the folklore existed. She was familiar with the speech and manners of the region.

When she boarded the train in New York bound for Florida, she felt happy to be going home again. She had not been back since her days with the traveling theater company. And even though the intervening years had been hard ones, she had survived, triumphed even. So she watched the countryside roll past with the same eagerness she had felt as a child looking out the window on her first train ride. Only this time, she was going home.

On the way she stopped in Memphis, Tennessee, to see her brother Ben. But as the train pulled into the station, she caught a glimpse of Bob waiting on the platform, and it scared her for a moment. She was afraid he might still be hurt or angry at the way she had left his house in Florida so many years before. The train huffed to a stop, and she gathered her bags and moved to the doorway. As she stepped down onto the platform, Bob looked into her eyes and smiled so brightly all her worries vanished and she rushed forward into his arms. All was forgiven, on both sides.

But then he gave her the bad news. Papa had been killed in an automobile accident several years before. When Zora heard the words she suddenly felt so weak she had to sit down at once. Even though she had given up on ever getting along with Papa, she hadn't wanted him to die! She felt a lump in her throat, and the world suddenly seemed dreary. Bob put his arm around her and tried to comfort her. Papa and their stepmother had divorced, he said. And Papa had begun to realize the sorrows he had caused his children. But Zora just kept thinking how she was really an orphan now. And a heavy door seemed to close inside her.

At Ben's they talked about the rest of the family. Ben himself was a pharmacist in Memphis and Joel a school principal in Alabama. John owned a market in Jacksonville, where Zora was headed. Dick was a chef but never stayed in one place too long. Everett, the baby, lived in Brooklyn just across the river from Zora. And Sarah was married and still in south central Florida.

A few days later Zora left Memphis and continued south. She planned to begin collecting folklore in Jacksonville and work her way down to Eatonville. She had six months to gather all the folklore she could manage, although she had to report regularly to Boas, who was overseeing the expedition from New York.

It was unusual for a person fresh out of college to be given such an opportunity. Most young folklorists had to work with older, more experienced scientists for several years before getting a chance to travel across the country alone. Zora knew she was being given a special opportunity, mostly because of Franz Boas' trust in her ability. And it was important to her. For many years she had survived without anybody's help. Many days she found it hard to even believe in herself. Boas' faith seemed to stir her own confidence. Both he and Zora were excited about her chances of discovering new information. Since she was black, it would be easier for her to fit in than it had been for the few white folklorists who had gone before. So she set off with high hopes. With any luck, at her young age, she might become the country's leading authority on black folklore.

For several weeks before her departure, she and Papa Franz had carefully gone over the requirements of the job. Collecting folklore is not as easy as it may seem. It is more than copying down a story or a song. Zora had to pay attention to the way the story was told. She had to memorize the gestures the storyteller used, the tone of voice, and the way the storyteller stood or sat. And she had to collect whatever she could get — whether she liked the stories and songs or not. Then she had to study them closely. Part of her job was determining what made the folklore unique. If it was a song, she compared it to songs from different cultures and to other songs she had collected in the same region.

In most of the towns she visited, Zora was a complete stranger. She had to get to know people as quickly as possible so they would begin to relax around her. If she stood out too much, if she seemed too different, they probably wouldn't give her any information.

From the start things went badly. Even Zora's easy

manner and knowledge of the region did not seem to help very much. The people she met stared at her with suspicion. And when she asked them for folktales and songs, they just shook their heads and sent her further down the road.

Zora was baffled. At first she thought the folklore she had come to collect had already disappeared. The black men and women she encountered seemed more interested in contemporary jazz records than in traditional stories and songs. Even Eatonville was a disappointment. The home folks were nice to her, but nobody had much to say, even at Joe Clarke's store.

Zora began to panic. Boas had put his trust in her, and now this! Even the few stories she did manage to collect had already been gathered by other folklorists. When she sent them to Boas, he was disappointed and said so. It got so bad Zora had trouble sleeping. She kept dreaming about Boas' sad, discouraged eyes. Her hopes for the future seemed to be slipping away.

Years later, after several successful expeditions, Zora began to understand the reasons her first trip went so badly. The biggest problems were her attitude and speech. Without meaning to, she had gone back to Florida sounding too much like an outsider, enunciating her words clearly in the Barnard College way instead of talking in the relaxed speech of a native. "I didn't go back there so that the home folks could make admiration over me because I had been up North to college," she wrote. "I needed my Barnard education to help me see my people as they really are. But I found that it did not do to be too detached as I stepped aside to study them. I had to go back, dress as they did, talk as they did, live their life, so that I could get...the world I knew as a child."

The expedition wasn't a complete failure. She did collect some new material. She also became fascinated by black magic, or "hoodoo" as it is called in the South, and made up her mind to find out more about it when she had the chance. And she traveled to Alabama to visit Cudjo Lewis, the last known survivor of a slave ship. He had been captured as a young boy in Africa and sold as a slave in the United States. Zora made his acquaintance but could only interview him briefly, since she had a pressing appointment to keep in Florida.

In the years since Eatonville, Zora had become a lovely young woman. She was slender but strong, with a clear oval face and light brown skin. Her mouth was wide and quick to laugh. And her eyes were like her mother's: dark and deep. In May, she took a break from collecting and headed to St. Augustine, Florida, to see Herbert Sheen, whom she had met at Howard University six years before. He was studying to become a doctor. Besides being a very good student, he could play piano and sing and dance. The two had fallen in love almost at once and stayed close over the years and miles that passed between them. After their reunion in Florida, they decided to get married. So they bought their licenses and went to City Hall to tie the knot.

But instead of boosting her spirits, the marriage added new burdens. During the 1920s and 30s, few women had careers outside the home. Most who did were expected to give them up after marriage. But Zora's career had just begun! And since she was not willing to stop collecting and follow her husband to Chicago, the couple soon parted. When she returned to New York at the end of her expedition, she was alone and full of disappointment. For all practical purposes her marriage was already over. And though she had collected some new material, it didn't meet her expectations. "Oh, I got a few items,"she wrote. "But compared with what I did later, not enough to make a flea a waltzing jacket."

13

Godmother

Soon after Zora returned to New York, she was introduced to an elderly white woman named Charlotte Mason, who had a lot of money. Sometimes Mrs. Mason gave money to artists she considered talented. Zora was anxious to meet her. She wanted to go south again, and she needed cash to do it.

Since Mrs. Mason was very wealthy, she was used to having her way. She was used to sitting up in her lavish apartment on Park Avenue and directing the goings-on of people around her. But she also had a passion for anthropology and was very well educated. And she had lived for a time among the Plains Indians collecting folklore. Since they had so much in common, Zora and Mrs. Mason hit it off at once. Soon they became very close — so close Zora began calling the older woman "Godmother."

The name was fitting. In many ways Mrs. Mason was like a fairy godmother, waving her magic wand across Zora's life. Until she met the older woman, bills and money matters seemed to demand most of Zora's time and attention, while writing and folklore had to wait. Godmother's money would make many new things possible. But as Zora soon discovered, Mrs. Mason had a dark side, too.

"Godmother could be as tender as mother-love when she felt that you had been right spiritually," Zora explained.

"But anything in you, however clever, that felt like insincerity to her called forth her well-known 'That is nothing! It has no soul in it.'"

Zora was like Godmother in many ways. For one thing, she could be very stubborn. And she was strong-tempered and outgoing. The women also shared an interest in the supernatural and were anxious to learn more about hoodoo in the South. And they had friends in common. One of Godmother's closest advisors was Alain Locke, whom Zora had met at Howard University. Mrs. Mason consulted him whenever she had a decision to make about the black artists she supported. One of these artists was Langston Hughes, a young poet Zora had known for several years.

Zora's relationship with Godmother was complicated. Like water from the tap, it ran either hot or cold. When Zora grew interested in things outside folklore, Godmother became cold and disapproving. But as long as Zora was busy collecting folktales, Godmother was happy. She wanted to hear all about the things Zora discovered. As Zora explained, "I must tell the tales, sing the songs, do the dances, and report the raucous sayings and doings of the Negro farthest down. She is altogether in sympathy with them, because she says truthfully they are utterly sincere in living."

Three months after Zora was introduced to Godmother, the older woman came through: She agreed to give Zora money to go south again. In exchange, she wanted control of all the folklore Zora collected. If Zora wanted to publish any of it, she would have to get permission. And she had to promise to keep Godmother's name secret. To make sure Zora upheld her end of the bargain, Mrs. Mason had her sign a contract.

But Zora was glad to accept the agreement. Even though she was a little difficult, Godmother had always been honest and direct. So Zora signed the contract and boarded the train south again. This time her trip would be more successful.

14

"Lies"

She went back to Alabama first thing. Cudjo Lewis, the last slave boat survivor, was old and might die soon, and she wanted to talk to him again. Their first meeting had been awkward, and Zora had been rushed for time. To make matters worse, Lewis spoke with a heavy accent and sometimes his memory failed. She simply hadn't been prepared on her first expedition. But now she felt ready for anything.

She took more time with the old man, visiting him regularly over a period of several weeks. Some days he would be tired and have trouble remembering things. On others he spoke very truthfully about the horrors of his life as a slave, and his eyes would water as he stared into the distance. Then he would recall in vivid detail how he had been captured more than 60 years before.

His village had been attacked at dawn by warriors from a nearby city. Only the strong and healthy were kept alive to be sold as slaves. The rest of the village — the elderly and very young — were murdered immediately. After the attack, the warriors chained Cudjo and the other captives and marched them many miles to the coast, where slave traders waited to buy them. Cudjo was crammed onto a dirty ship bound for America, leaving forever his language, his country and his family. Sometimes he wept as he told Zora the story. She came away from the meetings near tears

herself, for all the anguish the old man had endured.

From Alabama, Zora headed to Florida, where she bought a car for her travels. She planned to spend some time in Eatonville, but she wanted to visit more remote parts of the state, too, even though it was a risk. Collecting folklore could be dangerous, especially for a woman traveling alone in the 1920s.

Most scientists believed that the purest folklore existed in isolated villages, where the townspeople had not been too heavily influenced by the outside world. So Zora looked for small, out-of-the-way places. Since she was a complete stranger, she had to live among her informants a while to win their trust. Cut off from the rest of the world, she was completely at their mercy. "I could have been maimed or killed on most any day of the several years of my research work," she explained. "Primitive minds are quick to sunshine and quick to anger. Some little word, look or gesture can move them either to love or to sticking a knife between your ribs."

Thirty miles south of Eatonville, in Florida's Polk County, Zora entered the Cypress Lumber camp and rented a room in one of the houses the company provided for its employees. The camp was one of the isolated communities Zora had hoped to find. Since it was a tightly knit neighborhood, word of her arrival spread fast. By evening most of the camp's inhabitants had found some excuse to drop by and check her out. It made her a little uneasy to see them eyeing her, but she just smiled and said hello.

For the next few days, everyone treated her politely, but she could tell they were wary. Whenever she entered a room, everyone stopped talking. She tried a few stories and jokes to loosen them up, but nothing seemed to work.

Since she had a car, she offered to drive one of the men into town for provisions one afternoon, and on the way he confided in her. Everybody suspected she was a police agent or informer, he said, because of her car and the city clothes she wore. Zora just laughed, but her mind was racing to think up a story to remedy the situation. What could she say to make them trust her? A little further down the road, she had an idea.

She pulled over and confessed the "truth," telling her passenger nervously that she was on the run from the police herself. She kept looking back over her shoulder as she talked, as though she expected to see a police car pull around the curve at any moment. Then she whispered that she had taken the car and the money for clothes from her boyfriend, who made illegal whiskey.

That evening, back at camp, Zora noticed a change. Instead of avoiding her company, several men approached and began kidding around. She laughed and exchanged jokes with them. Her story had spread through the camp. Apparently it had been believed. But she ordered some plain dresses at the company store anyway, to be safe.

It wasn't long before Zora decided to make friends with the biggest, strongest woman in the camp, a woman called "Big Sweet." She figured it would be wise to have a little muscle on her side, just in case. So when she passed Big Sweet on the road to town one day, she stopped and offered her a ride. Soon they were laughing down the highway together, exchanging compliments. By the time they got back to camp that evening, they were best friends.

And the friendship paid off. Whenever Zora needed material, Big Sweet herded a bunch of people together to tell stories, or "lies" as they called them. "I enjoyed collecting the folktales and I believe the people from whom I collected them enjoyed the telling of them, just as much as I did the hearing. Once they got started, the 'lies' just rolled and storytellers fought for a chance to talk. It was the same with the songs."

One day Zora decided to follow the men on the swamp crew to work and collect some of their songs and stories. So she went to bed early. The swamp crew rose before dawn and often worked long past dusk clearing the countryside of trees and thickets.

In the next day's early darkness, she was awakened by the hoarse voice of the "shack-rouser," who moved from hut to hut calling:

Wake up bullies, and git on de rock. 'Tain't quite daylight but it's four o'clock.

That was his first round. A little while later she heard him again. This time he was yelling:

Wake up, Jacob, day's a breakin'. Git yo' hoe-cake a bakin' and yo' shirt tail shakin'.

By then she could see lights in the windows dotting the camp and hear the clatter of breakfast dishes and lunch buckets. The men had worked their morning chores into a routine: *"Break your hoe-cake half in two. Half on the plate, half in the dinner-bucket. Throw in your black-eyed peas and fat meat left from supper and your bucket is fixed. Pour meat grease in your bread. A big bowl of coffee, a drink of water from the tin dipper in the pail. Grab your dinner-bucket and hit the grit. Don't keep the straw-boss waiting."*

In the swamp where the men worked all day, alligators lurked, and so did snakes and even panthers. A man alone wouldn't last very long, but the crew members looked out

for each other. It wasn't unusual to see a man suddenly straighten up, squint into the distance, and hurl his axe several yards into the skull of an alligator. The men moved like powerful but graceful machines, their sweaty backs glistening in the sun, their arms twirling the axes overhead before each downstroke.

At lunch the men leaned back in the shade of a tree and traded stories. In free moments like these, which were rare, they worked off steam by thinking of new ways to insult each other. On the day Zora accompanied the men, the boss was off tending to other business, so they decided to focus on him instead. One man said, *"I had a straw boss and he was so mean that when the boiler burst and blowed some of the men up in the air, he docked 'em for de time they was off de job."* Then somebody else joined in. *"Over on de East Coast Ah used to have a road boss and he was so mean and times was so hard till he laid off de hands of his watch."* They all laughed then, even Zora. In the lumber camps, the boss was never popular.

A few nights later Zora was almost killed in a knife fight. Even though most of the camp believed the story about her bootlegging boyfriend, a few remained skeptical, and most of them were women. One was jealous of the long hours Zora spent collecting stories among the men. So one night at a local party, she cornered Zora and pulled out a long, glimmering blade.

Luckily, Big Sweet was playing cards in a corner and saw the commotion. "Big Sweet yelled to me to run," Zora wrote. "I really ran, too. I ran out of the place, ran to my room, threw my things in the car and left the place. When the sun came up I was a hundred miles up the road."

15

Hoodoo

Godmother's support lasted three years. Zora spent most of that time collecting folklore and organizing her findings. When her attention wandered to other things, like theater or fiction writing, Godmother tightened her hold over Zora and threatened to cut off her money. But even after Godmother's support ended, as it eventually did, Zora continued to collect new material.

On her first expedition she had become interested in hoodoo, so she devoted a lot of time to it on later trips. In the South and across much of the West Indies, the belief in hoodoo was so widespread many people considered it a religion. They believed that a hoodoo doctor, sometimes called a conjure man or woman, had unusual powers that were triggered by certain formulas, chants, ceremonies and sometimes roots and herbs. Since hoodoo was a well-kept secret among believers, no one knew how many there were. But Zora was convinced that in the 1920s and 30s there were thousands, if not more.

Hoodoo didn't originate in the South, although it survives there even today. Anthropologists believe that many of its ceremonies come from Africa. Most scientists consider it a "sympathetic" magic, a kind of self-hypnosis where the believer hypnotizes himself into seeing the outcome he desires. But for the men and women who participate in hoodoo, it is anything but hypnosis. The hoodoo doctor performs many of the same jobs as priests, lawyers and medical doctors, only the hoodoo doctor is much more fearsome. Believers are convinced he can heal warts, break up love affairs, drive a person out of town, bring illness, even cause death. Although many people believe in the powers of hoodoo and turn to it for help, few ever learn its secrets. In her travels, Zora became one of those few.

In the late summer of 1928, she headed for New Orleans, the hoodoo capital of North America. Only one other folklorist had ever had any success studying hoodoo. He was a white man named Newbell Niles Puckett, who tried to obtain secrets by pretending to be a conjure man himself. Since most of his informants were black, and since hoodoo is such a well-guarded secret, it is unlikely that Puckett obtained very much authentic material. In fact, he was probably given false information to keep him out of the way.

When Zora arrived in New Orleans, she took a different approach. She asked the conjure men and women she discovered to let her be their apprentice. Since she was black, she passed the color barrier. Since she was a young woman asking to learn, not an older man pretending to compete, she gained their trust much more readily.

In New Orleans, a woman named Marie Leveau was considered the "queen" of hoodoo. Although she died many years before Zora arrived in the city, legends about her power were common. When Zora met a conjure man named Luke Turner who claimed to be her nephew, she heard many of these legends firsthand. "The police hear so much about Marie Leveau," he told her, "that they come to her house in St. Anne Street to put her in jail. First one come, she stretch out her left hand and he turn round and round and never stop until some one come lead him away. Then two come together — she put them to running and barking like dogs. Four come and she put them to beating each other with night sticks. The whole station force come. They knock at her door. She know who they are before she ever look. She did work at her altar and they all went to sleep on her steps."

Zora was a little frightened by what she learned in New Orleans. As an apprentice, she had to participate in the ceremonies of her teachers, and sometimes it meant gathering a handful of dirt from an old grave or drawing her own blood. There was a ritual in the woods where a wide circle was drawn around a fiery pot in which the bone of a black cat simmered. One conjure man slept in a coffin. Another had Zora lie face-down on a sofa for three days and nights without food or water.

Some of the things she encountered were familiar. She learned, for instance, that the spirit of a person who has just died can be destructive. That is the reason all clocks and mirrors in the room must be covered at death. If they aren't, the clock may be permanently broken, and the mirror may never reflect the faces of the living again. Was it all true? Zora didn't know. But the more she explored, the more mysterious were the things she discovered.

A few years later she sailed to the West Indies to find out more. In Haiti, some people believed there were hoodoo gods. Whenever they needed special help or a cure from illness, they turned to the proper god for the answer. Each god had special concerns. Some were good and asked only small sacrifices for their favors. Others were evil and vindictive. They granted special powers to people, but often the price for these powers was great. Zora crisscrossed the country studying these things.

One day, while she was visiting an American friend, a Haitian woman came running up to invite them to a special ceremony. At the ceremony, all the food would be cooked *without* fire. Naturally Zora and her friend were curious. They had never heard of such a thing. They asked the woman to repeat herself.

Instead she asked for several objects: a fresh egg, a cup and saucer, cold water, and laundry bluing. Zora's friend went inside the house and returned with the items. The woman placed the egg in the cup, poured cold water around it, and covered it with the saucer. With the bluing, she marked the saucer. Then she whispered a few words to herself. When she finished, she held out the egg to her friends and urged them to crack it open. To their amazement, the egg was thoroughly cooked!

Zora and her friend made up their minds to attend the ceremony the woman had mentioned. They traveled deep into the Haitian countryside, coming at last to a small clearing where a group of people had already gathered. Instead of a cup, a large pot stood in the clearing to hold all the food. When everything was ready, some men began to beat their drums and the people started to dance. They moved around the pot, waving hats and scarves. When they stopped, the food was steaming!

Zora tried everything she could think of to unravel the mystery. What was the secret? How did they do it? But no one would tell her. The power to cook without fire had come from the gods, the people said. If they passed the secret to anyone else, the punishment was death.

In her explorations, Zora came to the island of Nassau in the Bahamas and was instantly enchanted. "I loved the place the moment I landed," she wrote later. "That first night as I lay in bed, listening to the rustle of a cocoanut palm just outside my window, a song accompanied by string and drum broke out in full harmony....The song has a beautiful air, and the oddest rhythm.

Bellamina, Bellamina!
She come back in the harbor
Bellamina, Bellamina
She come back in the harbor
Put Bellamina on the dock
And paint Bellamina black! Black!
Oh, put the Bellamina on the dock
And paint Bellamina, black! Black!

She had come to study hoodoo, but discovered a wealth of song and dance. The island was rich with all three. Its inhabitants translated the simplest events into music, then acted them out in spectacular movements with their bodies. Even their speech was magical, full of soft, melodic cadences. And under the surface of everyday life, in the velvety black nights, hoodoo smoldered.

16

Storytelling

Down in Florida on one of her collecting trips, Zora discovered a guitar player like no other she had heard before. She had gone to collect some stories, but the guitar player soon chased them out of her mind. When he leaned over his "box" and started picking, Zora felt herself pulled inside the music. He could make that guitar laugh, talk, scream, whoop with joy and weep like the world was coming to an end. How could she describe that in an anthropology book?

It was impossible.

And in her father's church many years before, she had been thrilled by the full, throaty voices of the choir rising overhead and spilling through the cracks in the heavy double doors. Sometimes white folks would drop by the Macedonia Baptist Church for the Sunday service. But even as a child, Zora knew they hadn't come to hear her father preach, powerful as his sermons were. They had come for the music. How could she convey the songs in an article about folklore?

She couldn't.

When she headed to New York, where people had begun giving concerts of "real Negro music," she was even more bewildered. What she saw on the stage wasn't real, just a bunch of trained performers who had practiced their material so many times they had ruined it. "On the concert stage, I always heard songs called spirituals sung and applauded as Negro music," she wrote, "and I wondered what would happen if a white audience ever heard a real spiritual. To me, what the Negroes did in Macedonia Baptist Church was finer than anything that any trained composer had done to the folksongs."

It wasn't long before she began to turn away from anthropology and folklore. Science had helped her understand the importance of the stories and songs of her childhood. But it didn't help the world see her people as living, breathing men and women who worked, suffered and laughed like anyone else. It made them into scientific specimens and statistics.

She knew her people were strong and creative. How could she convince the world?

For answers, she turned to theater and fiction.

She wanted to put the songs she had collected on stage so people could hear for themselves how beautiful they were. Then, she was sure, they would feel the same way she did.

When she mentioned the idea to her friend Langston Hughes, he liked it so much he wanted to help. So they wrote a play together about Eatonville, and filled it with stories and songs. But then they began to argue over it, and the argument became so bitter the play was never produced.

But Zora was still determined. She organized a group of performers and prepared her own concert. With songs, stories and dance they acted out a typical day in the black South. Instead of dressing her performers in tuxedos and long gowns, as other concert directors did, she clothed them in Southern work clothes and Bahamian costumes. She didn't rehearse them in the usual way, either, but encouraged them to follow their natural inclinations. "Because I know that music without motion is not natural with my people, I did not have the singers stand in a stiff group and reach for the high note. I told them to just imagine that they were in Macedonia and go ahead."

She called her first show *The Great Day*, and in 1932 it opened for a one-night performance in New York City. The show was a hit. Zora had been right. People did appreciate real black music.

But it was her writing that conveyed the most about her people. After all, folks are usually best at the things they love most. From as far back as she could remember, there had been a store-porch full of talkers who translated the world around them into tales. The owls, the mules and even machines had stories told about them. The moon burning a path across the lake was really the pearly eye of a magical being, the soft rustling that moved through the trees the breath of angels.

And the characters in her short stories and novels were more complete than anything she might describe in a science journal. They were usually black. They lived in the South, typically Florida. They worked hard, laughed hard and cried hard. And when they talked to one another they used the clear, evocative speech of Joe Clarke's store porch.

Zora had been a good student, a gifted folklorist, a courageous conjure apprentice and a perceptive concert director. But she was a daughter of Eatonville, so her stories shone the brightest. And more than anything else, it was her storytelling that brought her fame.

17

Give Me a River

By 1943, when Zora was in her early 50s, she had become the leading black woman writer in America. She had published three novels, two books about folklore and hoodoo, and an autobiography. Her face had appeared on the cover of a popular magazine. Her autobiography had been cited for its contribution to racial harmony. Godmother had long since relinquished control of the folklore. And Zora had been awarded two fellowships from the Guggenheim Foundation.

But there was sadness in her life, too. Franz Boas was dead. And the United States was caught up in World War II, fighting to free Europe from Hitler.

Zora did her best to support her country in war, writing articles and speaking out against Hitler's murderous crimes. But she wondered when somebody was going to liberate the blacks at home. After all, Jim Crow was still the law of the land. The separate schools, hotels, water fountains and neighborhoods remained. White mobs continued to terrorize their black brothers. And most black children lived in poverty.

And though Zora was famous, she was beginning to draw a lot of criticism, too. Most famous people do. But Zora's case was unique because most of her critics were black.

Many of them believed the best way to escape racism was to adopt the ways of whites. That meant getting an education and a good job and avoiding anything that even hinted of their history as slaves. So when Zora wrote stories about the rural South, it made them angry. They wished she wouldn't emphasize the things that made them different.

Other blacks criticized her for different reasons. They thought her stories overlooked the horrible misery and violence blacks faced in the South. They wanted her to write about the crimes whites had committed against them. But most of her stories didn't even mention whites.

Not that whites understood her any better. They liked her stories but for the wrong reasons. They thought her characters were fascinating, but they didn't take them seriously. Instead, they continued to think of the black race as inferior.

Zora was caught in the crossfire, and it hurt. To her the truth was as plain as day: Blacks were different, and they should have been proud of their difference, not ashamed. They should like themselves and treat each other respectfully, whether white folks ever did or not.

And the war made things worse. It seemed to let a whirlwind of hate loose upon the land. Everywhere she went she encountered it, and it wasn't just racism. It was hate, pure and simple. Neighbors turned against neighbors, husbands and wives fought, and even strangers glared at each other with a cold, calculated passion. It got so bad she wouldn't leave her room in New York. Then she got sick, and it seemed she would never recuperate. Finally she turned to the only haven that remained — home.

She headed to Florida, where she bought a houseboat called the *Wanago*. In a matter of days she had loaded it with her belongings and set off to cruise the Indian and Halifax rivers. The warm sun and gentle waters helped lull her back to health. Most days she stayed in the boat's cabin and wrote. At night she sat on deck and watched the stars migrate across the sky. When she wanted to be lazy, she fished in the still waters or lay in the sun and feasted on oranges.

Across the ocean men were still murdering each other in war. And in America, misunderstanding prowled the land. It pained her to see the earth in such a state. But she had traveled far and worked hard and really loved her people. For this little bit of her life, these few years floating down the river, she was contented. She had her world, and for now, it was good.

Epilogue

Throughout her life Zora Neale Hurston continued to collect folklore and write, and remained dedicated to the theater as a forum for her material. During the 1930s, she directed a number of versions of *The Great Day* across the country.

In 1948, she published her last novel, then began to slip into poverty. When she died in 1960, in a welfare home in Florida, she was penniless.

Many of her personal belongings were burned after her death, including most of the manuscript she had been working on for several years. Her name was misspelled on her death certificate, and she was buried in an unmarked grave in a segregated cemetery. Her books went out of print. And the few existing copies became hard to find, even in libraries.

During the turbulent 1960s, dozens of black American authors were rediscovered and their books reprinted. Zora Hurston was not one of them. But in 1973, when Alice Walker wrote about her journey to Florida to mark Zora Hurston's grave, she sparked new interest in the writer.

Hurston's books were reissued, and have sold more copies in the years since her death than they did during her entire lifetime. In 1990, Hurston was inducted posthumously into the Florida Artists' Hall of Fame, and the town of Eatonville began an annual celebration of her life: the Zora Neale Hurston Festival of the Arts and Humanities.

And on Feb. 14, 1991, *Mule Bone*, the play Hurston had written 60 years before with Langston Hughes, opened for the first time in New York City.

Notes

The events in this book are based primarily on two texts: *Dust Tracks on a Road*, Hurston's award-winning autobiography; and *Zora Neale Hurston: A Literary Biography*, by Robert E. Hemenway. *Dust Tracks* contains vivid, poignant descriptions of Hurston's childhood and early adolescence in Eatonville, Florida, but reveals little about her adult life or her often tempestuous friendships and collaborations. Hemenway also describes Hurston's childhood, but goes on to give an in-depth portrayal of her later years, for which he interviewed friends, colleagues and family members and analyzed Hurston's writings: her correspondence, seven full-length books and more than 70 short stories, plays, and newspaper and magazine articles. The Hemenway biography also includes a comprehensive list of Hurston's fiction and nonfiction books, articles and other writings.

In the first six chapters of this book, some of the dialogue has been reconstructed, based on specific events and interpersonal exchanges described in Hurston's own account of her childhood.

The story of color included in Chapter 3 is also taken from *Dust Tracks* and is Hurston's version of an African-American folktale. The descriptions of "Old Death" excerpted in Chapter 4 were written by Hurston and published in *Dust Tracks*. The rest of the sayings and figures of speech printed in this biography were taken from *Mules and Men*, which contains the folktales and games Hurston collected during the late 1920s and early 30s, strung together with an appealing narrative describing her adventures.

Another important source for this book is Nathan Huggins' *The Harlem Renaissance*, which describes the explosive creativity that occurred in Harlem in the 1920s and explores American race relations with great sensitivity and insight. These and other sources are listed in the bibliography.

Bibliography

Hemenway, Robert E., *Zora Neale Hurston: A Literary Biography*, Urbana, Illinois: University of Illinois Press, 1977.

Huggins, Nathan, *The Harlem Renaissance*, New York: Oxford University Press, 1971.

Hurston, Zora Neale, "Art and Such," *Reading Black, Reading Feminist: A Critical Anthology*, ed. by Henry Louis Gates, Jr., New York: Meridian, 1990.

– *Dust Tracks on a Road: An Autobiography*, Philadelphia: J.B. Lippincott, 1942.

– *I Love Myself When I Am Laughing ... & Then Again When I Am Looking Mean and Impressive: A Zora Neale Hurston Reader*, ed. by Alice Walker, Old Westbury, New York: The Feminist Press, 1979.

– *Jonah's Gourd Vine*, Philadelphia: J.B. Lippincott, 1934.

– *Moses, Man of the Mountain*, Philadelphia: J.B. Lippincott, 1939.

– *Mules and Men*, Philadelphia: J.B. Lippincott, 1935.

– *The Sanctified Church*, ed. by Toni Cade Bambara, Berkeley: Turtle Island Foundation, 1981.

– *Seraph on the Suwanee*, New York: Charles Scribner's Sons, 1948.

– *Spunk: The Selected Short Stories of Zora Neale Hurston*, Berkeley: Turtle Island Foundation, 1985.

– *Tell My Horse*, Philadelphia: J.B. Lippincott, 1938.

– *Their Eyes Were Watching God*, Philadelphia: J.B. Lippincott, 1937.

Walker, Alice, "Looking for Zora" and "Zora Neale Hurston: A Cautionary Tale and a Partisan View," *In Search of Our Mothers' Gardens*, New York: Harcourt Brace Jovanovich, 1983.

Chronology

1891	*January 7.* Zora Neale Hurston is born in Eatonville, Florida, to Lucy Potts Hurston and John Hurston.
ca. 1904	Lucy Potts Hurston dies, and Zora leaves home soon after for Jacksonville, Florida. The exact dates of events in Zora's life during this period are sketchy until 1917.
1917-18	Zora attends Morgan College Academy in Baltimore and earns her high school diploma.
1918-24	Zora works and studies in Washington, D.C., taking jobs as a waitress, manicurist and maid, and attending Howard University.
1921	Zora publishes "John Redding Goes to Sea," her first story, at Howard University in the *Stylus*.
1925	Zora's story "Spunk" and play *Color Struck* win second place awards in a contest sponsored by *Opportunity* magazine. She attends the awards banquet in New York City.
1925-27	Zora studies anthropology in New York at Barnard College, where she meets Franz Boas.
1927	*February.* Zora begins her first folklore-collecting trip to Florida.
	May 19. Zora and Herbert Sheen are married.
	September. Zora meets Charlotte Mason, whom she comes to call "Godmother."
	December. After signing a contract with Godmother, Zora heads south again to collect folklore.
1928	Zora receives her B.A. degree from Barnard College.

1930	*May-June.* Zora and Langston Hughes collaborate on *Mule Bone*, a play.
1931	*February.* Zora and Hughes quarrel over authorship of *Mule Bone*, ending their friendship.
	July 7. Zora and Sheen divorce.
1932	*January 10. The Great Day* is performed in New York City. Over the next few years, Zora stages various versions of *The Great Day* in different parts of the country.
1934	*May. Jonah's Gourd Vine*, Zora's first novel, is published.
1935	*October. Mules and Men*, Zora's account of her folklore collecting in the South, is published.
1936	*March.* The Guggenheim Foundation awards Zora a grant to study West Indian hoodoo practices.
	April-September. Zora studies hoodoo and folklore in Jamaica.
	September. Zora travels to Haiti, where she writes her most famous novel, *Their Eyes Were Watching God*, in seven weeks.
1937	*September. Their Eyes Were Watching God* is published.
1938	*Tell My Horse*, Zora's account of life and hoodoo in Haiti and Jamaica, is published.
1939	*June.* Morgan State College awards Zora an honorary Doctor of Letters degree. Zora marries Albert Price III in Florida.
	November. Zora's third novel, *Moses, Man of the Mountain*, is published.
1940	*February.* Zora files for divorce.

1942	*November.* Zora's autobiography, *Dust Tracks on a Road,* is published.
1943	Zora leaves New York City for Florida, where she purchases a houseboat and sails the Halifax and Indian rivers.
	February. Dust Tracks wins the Anisfield-Wolf Book Award in Race Relations. Zora makes the cover of *Saturday Review.*
	March. Zora receives the Distinguished Alumni Award from Howard University.
	November. Zora is divorced from Price.
1947	Zora travels to British Honduras to study black communities, and writes *Seraph on the Suwanee.*
1948	*September.* Zora is arrested in New York and falsely accused of molesting a 10-year-old boy.
	October. Seraph on the Suwanee is published.
1949	*March.* The molestation case against Zora is dismissed.
1956	*May.* Zora is honored for "education and human relations" by Bethune-Cookman College.
1959	Zora has a stroke and eventually enters the St. Lucie County Welfare Home in Florida because she is unable to care for herself.
1960	*January 28.* Zora dies in the welfare home and is buried in an unmarked grave in Fort Pierce, Florida.
1973	*August.* Alice Walker travels to Florida and marks Zora's grave.

Index

J

K

L

M

N

O